INSTANT POT DOG FOOD COOKBOOK

Dr. Doris Meany

Disclaimer:

The content within this book is offered solely for general information purposes. The author and publisher disclaim any responsibility for actions taken in reliance on the material herein. Although every endeavor has been made to ensure the accuracy and comprehensiveness of the information, the author and publisher do not provide any explicit or implied guarantees regarding the reliability, appropriateness, or accessibility of the content contained in this book.

OTHER BOOKS BY THE AUTHOR

Slow Cooker Dog Food Cookbook

Homemade Dog Biscuit Cookbook

Homemade Dog Treats Using Baking Mats

IF YOU WOULD LIKE TO CHECK OUT MORE BOOKS BY DR.DORIS MEANY, SCAN THE QR CODE BELOW

TABLE OF CONTENTS

INTRODUCTION

In the silent moments just before dawn, when the world was draped in a hushed blanket of obsidian, I found myself in the gentle embrace of solitude. It was during these moments, as the world stirred reluctantly awake, that I'd often reflect upon the intricate tapestry of my life. And amongst the threads that wove through the fabric of my existence, there was one undeniable truth—a truth that sparked a journey that would forever change not just my own life, but the lives of countless others and their furry companions.

As a fervent lover of all things canine, my life's purpose seemed written in the loving gazes of the pets I'd cared for over the past two decades. With each wagging tail, soulful eyes, and tender nuzzle, my resolve to provide the best possible care for these cherished creatures strengthened. Yet, despite my professional expertise as a seasoned veterinary dietician, an unexpected and transformative moment loomed in my path.

It was a day etched in my memory like an indelible ink stain on a blank canvas. A day when the fragility of life stared me in the face, demanding attention and change. A day when a seemingly innocent dog treat, purchased with love and trust, almost became the inadvertent harbinger of tragedy for my beloved canine companion.

The aftermath was a turbulent whirlwind of frantic vet visits, prayers whispered through tears, and a solemn vow etched deep within my heart. I refused to let my fur-baby's life be a casualty of uncertainty or a product of commercially manufactured uncertainty. That moment marked a turning point—an awakening that propelled me onto a path less traveled.

Fuelled by a relentless determination to safeguard not only my own dog but also the countless others under my care, I embarked on a quest to revolutionize their dining experience. No longer content with the ambiguity that shrouded store-bought dog foods, I ventured into uncharted territory—into the heart of my own kitchen.

With a heavy heart and a fervent desire to right the wrongs inflicted upon my dear companion, I bid farewell to the aisles of expensive, questionable dog food. Instead, armed with determination and a yearning for change, I embraced a newfound sense of purpose—a mission to craft nourishment that would not only satiate hunger but nurture life itself.

My culinary odyssey led me through a labyrinth of recipes, trials, and discoveries. Yet, amidst this exploration, one tool emerged as a beacon of efficiency and innovation—the Instant Pot. As a professional balancing the demands of a bustling career and a love for my pets, this device became my trusted ally. Its seamless marriage of speed and nutrition offered a lifeline in the midst of my chaotic schedule.

The concoctions that bubbled and simmered within this modern marvel of culinary technology were not just meals but expressions of love, care, and dedication. Witnessing the unbridled joy in my dog's eyes as she savored these homemade delicacies stirred emotions that defied description.

Each experimental batch, meticulously perfected through trial and error, resonated not just with my furry friend's taste buds but also with her health. These nourishing creations served as a testament to the transformative power of homemade meals— crafted with the precision of a seasoned dietician and the heart of a devoted pet parent.

In the quietude of my kitchen, I'd unlocked a treasure trove of recipes that not only delighted my dog but also addressed specific health concerns. And as the aroma of wholesome ingredients wafted through my home, an unexpected chorus of curious clients and fellow pet lovers gathered around, eager to partake in this culinary revolution.

Their fervent requests for recipes tailored to their pets' unique dietary needs echoed a collective longing for change. It was in these moments of sharing, teaching, and connecting with like-minded souls that the seed of an idea began to germinate—a seed that would blossom into the very book you hold in your hands.

The decision to encapsulate these culinary adventures into a comprehensive guide, brimming with tantalizing recipes and insightful tips, didn't stem solely from a desire to share knowledge. It sprouted from a heartfelt yearning to empower every dog owner worldwide—to liberate them from the shackles of uncertainty and exorbitant expenses associated with commercial dog foods.

Within the pages of this book lie not just recipes, but a narrative of love, resilience, and a promise—a promise to enrich the lives of our furry companions in the most fundamental way possible—through nourishment that's not just food, but a manifestation of unwavering devotion.

So, to all fellow dog lovers, pet parents, and those seeking a healthier, more fulfilling journey alongside their faithful companions, I invite you to embark on this culinary expedition with me. Together, let's unleash the potential of homemade Instant Pot dog food, creating a symphony of flavors that harmonize with our dogs' health and happiness.

Join me as we delve into the chapters that follow—a tapestry woven with delectable recipes, practical guidance, and the shared passion for transforming mealtimes into moments of joy and well-being for our beloved pets. Welcome to the wondrous world of *Instant Pot Dog Food Cookbook*.

This is not just a book; it's a celebration—a celebration of the bond between humans and dogs, united by a common thread of love, care, and the desire to provide nothing but the best. Let us embark on this journey together, enriching the lives of our furry companions one meal at a time.

CHAPTER 1
BASICS OF DOG NUTRITION

UNDERSTANDING YOUR DOG'S NUTRITIONAL NEEDS

Welcome to the beginning of your journey into the world of crafting homemade meals for your furry companion using the incredible Instant Pot. In this chapter, we will delve into the fundamental aspects of dog nutrition, empowering you with essential knowledge to ensure your beloved pet's health and well-being through carefully curated meals.

Just as our own bodies require a balanced diet for optimal health, our canine friends also depend on a well-rounded nutritional intake to thrive. As a responsible pet owner, comprehending your dog's nutritional needs is pivotal in providing them with meals that support their growth, maintain their overall health, and enhance their quality of life.

Your dog's dietary requirements are influenced by various factors, including their breed, size, age, activity level, and specific health conditions. To ensure you meet these needs effectively, it's crucial to understand the essential nutrients that form the building blocks of a healthy canine diet.

ESSENTIAL NUTRIENTS FOR DOGS

1. Proteins: Often referred to as the "building blocks" of life, proteins play a vital role in your dog's diet. These nutrients are comprised of amino acids, which aid in muscle development, tissue repair, and the overall maintenance of a robust immune system. High-quality sources of protein include lean meats (such as chicken, turkey, beef, and lamb), fish, eggs, and dairy products.

2. Carbohydrates: While dogs are primarily carnivores, they can benefit from the energy derived from carbohydrates. Opt for whole grains like brown rice, quinoa, and oats as these provide sustained energy and dietary fiber, aiding in digestion and maintaining healthy bowel movements.

3. Fats: Healthy fats are a concentrated source of energy for dogs and are crucial for the absorption of fat-soluble vitamins. Omega-3 and Omega-6 fatty acids, found in sources like fish oil, flaxseed, and certain oils (like olive oil), support your dog's skin health, coat shine, and overall well-being.

4. Vitamins: Essential vitamins like A, B, C, D, and E are imperative for various bodily functions in dogs. They contribute to vision, bone health, immune function, and overall vitality. Incorporating a diverse range of fruits, vegetables, and supplements (if necessary) can help meet these requirements.

5. Minerals: Calcium, phosphorus, potassium, magnesium, and others are essential minerals vital for bone health, nerve function, muscle contraction, and enzymatic reactions. Natural sources include dairy products, leafy greens, and certain meats.

Balancing these nutrients in your dog's diet is key to maintaining their optimal health. However, achieving this balance isn't just about including these components; it's about ensuring the right proportions and variety in their meals.

COMMON INGREDIENTS IN HOMEMADE DOG FOOD

Now that you're familiar with the essential nutrients, let's explore the common ingredients used in preparing homemade dog food. Crafting meals for your canine companion allows for greater control over ingredients and can steer clear of the uncertainties found in some commercial dog foods.

1. Lean Meats: Chicken, turkey, beef, and lamb serve as excellent sources of protein. Always choose lean cuts, removing excess fat and bones before preparing the meat.

2. Fish: Certain fish varieties, such as salmon and mackerel, are rich in Omega-3 fatty acids, benefiting your dog's skin, coat, and overall health. Ensure the fish is deboned and thoroughly cooked to avoid any potential hazards.

3. Vegetables: Incorporating a colorful array of vegetables—such as carrots, sweet potatoes, green beans, peas, and spinach—provides essential vitamins and minerals. Be sure to chop or puree them to make digestion easier for your furry friend.

4. Fruits: Apples, bananas, blueberries, and strawberries are among the fruits that can offer added nutrients and natural sweetness to your dog's meals. Remove seeds and pits before feeding them to your pet.

5. Whole Grains: Brown rice, quinoa, and oats serve as wholesome sources of carbohydrates and fiber. These grains contribute to energy levels and aid in maintaining a healthy digestive system for your dog.

6. Eggs: Eggs are a powerhouse of nutrients, providing protein, vitamins, and minerals. They can be a beneficial addition to your dog's diet when cooked thoroughly.

When preparing homemade dog food, always ensure that ingredients are cooked thoroughly to avoid any potential risks associated with raw food. Additionally, consult with your veterinarian to determine portion sizes and ensure your recipes align with your dog's specific nutritional needs.

By understanding your dog's nutritional requirements and familiarizing yourself with these common ingredients, you are laying a solid foundation for crafting nutritious and delectable meals using the Instant Pot. This knowledge equips you to create a diverse range of recipes tailored to your furry friend's tastes and health needs.

In the chapters that follow, we will explore the art of utilizing the Instant Pot to create an array of wholesome, homemade dog food recipes that will undoubtedly delight your dog's palate while ensuring their well-being. So, buckle up and get ready to embark on an exciting culinary adventure that will deepen the bond between you and your cherished pet.

CHAPTER 2
INSTANT POT BASICS

Welcome to the heart of your culinary journey—the Instant Pot. In this chapter, we'll embark on an exploration of this remarkable kitchen appliance, unraveling its secrets, and equipping you with the knowledge needed to harness its full potential in creating nourishing meals for your beloved canine companion.

GETTING STARTED WITH YOUR INSTANT POT

The Instant Pot stands as a modern marvel, a multifunctional device that amalgamates various cooking methods into one streamlined appliance. From pressure cooking and sautéing to steaming and slow cooking, its versatility is unparalleled. To commence your journey with the Instant Pot, let's navigate through the initial steps:

1. Familiarization: Take a moment to acquaint yourself with the components of your Instant Pot. From the stainless-steel inner pot to the lid, sealing ring, and control panel—each element serves a crucial purpose in the cooking process.

2. Assembling: Begin by placing the inner pot inside the Instant Pot base. Ensure it's properly seated and secure before proceeding.

3. Sealing: Before cooking, it's essential to ensure the sealing ring is correctly fitted within the lid's grooves. This rubber ring plays a pivotal role in maintaining pressure during cooking.

4. Testing: Conduct a water test to familiarize yourself with the Instant Pot's functionalities. Add water to the inner pot, secure the lid, and select the 'Pressure Cook' function. This test run helps verify the appliance's sealing and pressure buildup.

TIPS AND TRICKS FOR USING THE INSTANT POT

Now that you've acquainted yourself with the basics, let's delve into some tips and tricks to maximize your Instant Pot experience:

1. Understand Cooking Times: The Instant Pot reduces cooking times significantly compared to conventional methods. However, each recipe and ingredient may require different cooking durations. Refer to recipes or guidelines to determine appropriate cooking times.

2. Utilize the Saute Function: The Saute function allows for pre-cooking steps such as browning meat or sautéing vegetables directly in the Instant Pot before commencing pressure cooking. This function adds depth of flavor to your dishes.

3. Release Methods: Familiarize yourself with the two primary pressure release methods—the Natural Release (allowing pressure to subside naturally) and the Quick Release (manually releasing pressure using the valve). Different recipes may require specific release methods.

4. Liquid Requirements: Adequate liquid is essential for the Instant Pot to reach and maintain pressure. Ensure you follow recommended liquid quantities in recipes to prevent burns and ensure proper cooking.

5. Layer Ingredients Thoughtfully: Layering ingredients strategically can prevent burning and facilitate even cooking. Place denser items at the bottom and lighter ingredients on top to promote efficient heat distribution.

SAFETY PRECAUTIONS AND GUIDELINES

Safety remains paramount when using the Instant Pot. Adhering to safety precautions ensures not only your well-being but also the longevity of your appliance:

1. Ventilation: Ensure there's ample space around the Instant Pot to allow proper ventilation during operation. Avoid placing it under cabinets or in confined spaces.

2. Lid Safety: Always ensure the sealing ring is in good condition and properly fitted within the lid's grooves. A damaged or misplaced sealing ring may compromise the pressure-cooking process.

3. Pressure Release: Exercise caution when releasing pressure. Use oven mitts or a long-handled utensil to avoid direct contact with steam, and never obstruct the steam release valve.

3. Cleaning and Maintenance: Regularly clean the Instant Pot's components, including the sealing ring and steam release valve, to prevent food residues and ensure optimal performance. Refer to the manufacturer's guidelines for specific cleaning instructions.

4. Overfilling: Avoid overfilling the Instant Pot beyond its recommended capacity, as this may impede proper pressure buildup and cause spills or burns.

By familiarizing yourself with these Instant Pot basics, tips, and safety guidelines, you're poised to embark on a safe, efficient, and rewarding culinary adventure. The Instant Pot is not just a cooking appliance—it's a versatile tool that streamlines the process of preparing nourishing and flavorful meals for your furry friend.

.

NOTE FROM THE AUTHOR!

Hello there, before we dive into the next chapter, I want to extend my heartfelt gratitude to you for joining me on this remarkable journey. Exploring the realm of homemade dog food and nutrition can spark curiosity and raise questions. As a fellow dog lover, I'm here to be your guiding light.

Your decision to invest in this book means everything to me. I'm dedicated to supporting you at every turn. Whether you seek clarity, guidance, or a deeper understanding, don't hesitate to reach out via email at: **drdorismeanyvet@gmail.com**

I promise to personally respond within 24 hours, eager to assist as you strive for improved wellness. Your feedback and questions are immensely valuable. I genuinely appreciate the privilege of accompanying you through this process.

CHAPTER 3
HOMEMADE DOG FOOD RECIPES

POULTRY DELIGHTS

1) Chicken and Sweet Potato Stew

Cook Time: 25 minutes

Servings: 4

Ingredients:

- 1 pound boneless, skinless chicken thighs, diced
- 2 sweet potatoes, peeled and chopped
- 1 cup green beans, trimmed and chopped
- 2 cups low-sodium chicken broth
- 1 teaspoon dried parsley
- 1/2 teaspoon turmeric

Instructions:

1) Place diced chicken, sweet potatoes, and green beans into the Instant Pot.
2) Pour in chicken broth and sprinkle with parsley and turmeric.
3) Close the lid, set to high pressure for 8 minutes, then perform a quick release.
4) Once done, allow it to cool before serving.

Nutritional Information: (per serving)

Calories: 280 | Protein: 25g | Fat: 7g | Carbohydrates: 25g | Fiber: 4g

Tips:

- Adjust spices to your dog's preferences.
- Use organic ingredients when possible for added nutritional benefits.

2) Turkey and Quinoa Bowl

Cook Time: 20 minutes

Servings: 3

Ingredients:

- 1 pound ground turkey
- 1 cup quinoa, rinsed
- 1 carrot, shredded
- 1 zucchini, diced
- 2 cups low-sodium chicken broth
- 1 teaspoon dried oregano

Instructions:

1) Set the Instant Pot to sauté mode and cook ground turkey until browned.
2) Add quinoa, carrot, zucchini, chicken broth, and oregano to the pot.
3) Close the lid, set to high pressure for 5 minutes, then perform a quick release.
4) Stir well before serving.

Nutritional Information: (per serving)

Calories: 320 | Protein: 25g | Fat: 9g | Carbohydrates: 30g | Fiber: 5g

Tips:

- Use ground turkey with a lower fat content for a leaner option.
- Ensure the quinoa is well-rinsed to remove bitterness.

3) Chicken and Brown Rice Casserole

Cook Time: 22 minutes

Servings: 5

Ingredients:

- 1 pound boneless, skinless chicken breasts, cubed
- 1 cup brown rice, rinsed
- 1 bell pepper, diced
- 1 cup low-sodium chicken broth
- 1/2 teaspoon dried thyme

Instructions:

1) Place chicken, brown rice, bell pepper, chicken broth, and thyme into the Instant Pot.
2) Close the lid, set to high pressure for 10 minutes, then allow natural pressure release for 10 minutes.
3) Fluff the mixture gently with a fork before serving.

Nutritional Information: (per serving)

Calories: 270 | Protein: 25g | Fat: 3g | Carbohydrates: 30g | Fiber: 4g

Tips:

- Use brown rice for its higher nutritional value compared to white rice.
- Feel free to add other dog-safe vegetables your pup enjoys.

4) Chicken and Pumpkin Stew

Cook Time: 20 minutes

Servings: 4

Ingredients:

- 1 pound boneless, skinless chicken thighs, cut into chunks
- 1 cup pumpkin puree
- 1 cup green peas (frozen or fresh)
- 2 cups low-sodium chicken broth
- 1/2 teaspoon ground ginger
- 1/4 teaspoon cinnamon

Instructions:

1) Add chicken, pumpkin puree, green peas, chicken broth, ginger, and cinnamon to the Instant Pot.
2) Close the lid, set to high pressure for 6 minutes, then perform a quick release.
3) Allow it to cool slightly before serving.

Nutritional Information: (per serving)

Calories: 240 | Protein: 22g | Fat: 5g | Carbohydrates: 20g | Fiber: 5g

Tips:

- Ensure the pumpkin puree is plain without any added sugar or spices.
- Use fresh, cooked pumpkin if available for added texture.

5) Turkey and Spinach Meatballs

Cook Time: 15 minutes

Servings: 6

Ingredients:

- 1 pound ground turkey
- 1 cup spinach, finely chopped
- 1/2 cup rolled oats
- 1 egg
- 1/2 teaspoon dried basil
- 1/4 teaspoon black pepper

Instructions:

1) In a bowl, mix together ground turkey, chopped spinach, oats, egg, basil, and black pepper.
2) Form small meatballs and place them in the Instant Pot.
3) Close the lid, set to high pressure for 5 minutes, then perform a quick release.
4) Allow the meatballs to cool before serving.

Nutritional Information: (per serving)

Calories: 180 | Protein: 20g | Fat: 8g | Carbohydrates: 6g | Fiber: 2g

Tips:

- Use baby spinach for a milder flavor that dogs often prefer.
- Freeze any leftovers for future quick meals.

6) Chicken and Carrot Soup

Cook Time: 18 minutes

Servings: 4

Ingredients:

- 1 pound boneless, skinless chicken breasts, sliced
- 2 carrots, sliced
- 1 celery stalk, chopped
- 4 cups low-sodium chicken broth
- 1/2 teaspoon dried rosemary
- 1/4 teaspoon turmeric

Instructions:

1) Place chicken, carrots, celery, chicken broth, rosemary, and turmeric into the Instant Pot.
2) Close the lid, set to high pressure for 8 minutes, then perform a quick release.
3) Allow it to cool slightly before serving.

Nutritional Information: (per serving)

Calories: 220 | Protein: 24g | Fat: 4g | Carbohydrates: 14g | Fiber: 3g

Tips:

- Turmeric provides anti-inflammatory benefits for dogs.
- Adjust the texture by blending part of the soup for pickier eaters.

7) Turkey and Brown Rice Congee

Cook Time: 20 minutes

Servings: 4

Ingredients:

- 1 pound ground turkey
- 1 cup brown rice, rinsed
- 6 cups low-sodium chicken broth
- 1-inch piece ginger, grated

Instructions:

1) Brown ground turkey using the sauté function in the Instant Pot.
2) Add brown rice, chicken broth and grated ginger
3) Close the lid, set to high pressure for 12 minutes, then allow natural pressure release for 5 minutes.
4) Stir well before serving, garnishing with the remaining green onions.

Nutritional Information: (per serving)

Calories: 300 | Protein: 28g | Fat: 6g | Carbohydrates: 30g | Fiber: 3g

Tips:

- Congee offers a comforting texture for dogs recovering from illnesses.
- Adjust the amount of ginger based on your dog's taste preferences.

8) Chicken and Broccoli Casserole

Cook Time: 25 minutes

Servings: 5

Ingredients:

- 1 pound boneless, skinless chicken thighs, cubed
- 2 cups broccoli florets
- 1 cup brown rice, rinsed
- 2 cups low-sodium chicken broth
- 1/2 teaspoon garlic powder
- 1/4 teaspoon dried thyme

Instructions:

1) Place chicken, broccoli, brown rice, chicken broth, garlic powder, and thyme into the Instant Pot.
2) Close the lid, set to high pressure for 10 minutes, then allow natural pressure release for 10 minutes.
3) Mix gently before serving.

Nutritional Information: (per serving)

Calories: 280 | Protein: 24g | Fat: 6g | Carbohydrates: 28g | Fiber: 4g

Tips:

- Steam broccoli separately for a crisper texture if your dog prefers.
- Ensure the chicken is thoroughly cooked to prevent any risks.

9) Chicken and Pea Risotto

Cook Time: 22 minutes

Servings: 4

Ingredients:

- 1 pound boneless, skinless chicken breasts, diced
- 1 cup arborio rice
- 1 cup frozen peas
- 3 cups low-sodium chicken broth
- 1/2 teaspoon dried thyme
- 1/4 teaspoon black pepper

Instructions:

1) Place diced chicken, arborio rice, frozen peas, chicken broth, thyme, and black pepper into the Instant Pot.
2) Close the lid, set to high pressure for 6 minutes, then perform a quick release.
3) Allow it to rest for a few minutes before serving.

Nutritional Information: (per serving)

Calories: 310 | Protein: 28g | Fat: 3g | Carbohydrates: 40g | Fiber: 3g

Tips:

- Stir well after cooking for a creamy texture.
- Opt for low-sodium chicken broth to control sodium intake.

10) Turkey and Carrot Omelet

Cook Time: 15 minutes

Servings: 3

Ingredients:

- 1 cup ground turkey
- 3 eggs
- 1 carrot, grated
- 1/4 cup shredded cheese (optional)
- 1/2 teaspoon dried parsley
- 1/4 teaspoon turmeric

Instructions:

1) Set the Instant Pot to sauté mode and cook ground turkey until browned.
2) In a bowl, whisk eggs, then add grated carrot, cooked turkey, cheese (if using), parsley, and turmeric.
3) Pour the egg mixture into a greased heatproof dish that fits inside the Instant Pot.
4) Add 1 cup of water to the Instant Pot, place the dish on the trivet, and lower it into the pot.
5) Close the lid, set to high pressure for 7 minutes, then perform a quick release.
6) Allow the omelet to cool before serving.

Nutritional Information: (per serving)

Calories: 210 | Protein: 20g | Fat: 12g | Carbohydrates: 5g | Fiber: 1g

Tips:

- Customize with your dog's favorite vegetables.
- Ensure the omelette is cooked through before serving.

BEEFY GOODNESS

11) Beef and Rice Stew

Cook Time: 25 minutes

Servings: 4

Ingredients:

- 1 pound beef stew meat, cubed
- 1 cup brown rice, rinsed
- 2 cups low-sodium beef broth
- 1 teaspoon dried thyme
- 1/2 teaspoon paprika

Instructions:

1) Place beef, brown rice, beef broth, thyme, and paprika into the Instant Pot.
2) Close the lid, set to high pressure for 12 minutes, then perform a quick release.
3) Stir gently before serving.

Nutritional Information: (per serving)

Calories: 340 | Protein: 28g | Fat: 10g | Carbohydrates: 30g | Fiber: 4g

Tips:

- Use brown rice for added fiber and nutrients.
- Adjust seasoning according to your dog's taste preferences.

12)   Beef and Veggie Medley

Cook Time: 20 minutes

Servings: 5

Ingredients:

- 1 pound beef sirloin, thinly sliced
- 2 cups mixed vegetables (carrots, peas, green beans)
- 1 cup low-sodium beef broth
- 1 tablespoon olive oil
- 1/4 teaspoon dried rosemary

Instructions:

1) Set the Instant Pot to sauté mode and sear beef slices in olive oil until browned.
2) Add mixed vegetables, beef broth, and dried rosemary to the pot.
3) Close the lid, set to high pressure for 5 minutes, then perform a quick release.
4) Allow it to cool slightly before serving.

Nutritional Information: (per serving)

Calories: 280 | Protein: 26g | Fat: 8g | Carbohydrates: 20g | Fiber: 5g

Tips:

- Opt for a variety of colorful vegetables for nutritional diversity.
- Adjust cooking time based on your dog's preferred vegetable texture.

13) Beef and Lentil Curry

Cook Time: 30 minutes

Servings: 4

Ingredients:

- 1 pound beef stew meat, cubed
- 1 cup dried green lentils, rinsed
- 1 can (14 oz) coconut milk
- 1 tablespoon curry powder

Instructions:

1) Place beef, green lentils, coconut milk, and curry powder into the Instant Pot.
2) Close the lid, set to high pressure for 15 minutes, then perform a quick release.
3) Stir gently before serving.

Nutritional Information: (per serving)

Calories: 380 | Protein: 30g | Fat: 18g | Carbohydrates: 25g | Fiber: 10g

Tips:

- Choose lean cuts of beef for a healthier option.
- Adjust the spice level by altering the amount of curry powder.

14)   Beef and Potato Stew

Cook Time: 25 minutes

Servings: 4

Ingredients:

- 1 pound beef chuck roast, cubed
- 2 potatoes, peeled and cubed
- 1 cup beef bone broth
- 1 carrot, diced
- 1 celery stalk, chopped
- 1 teaspoon dried thyme

Instructions:

1) Place beef, potatoes, carrot, celery, beef bone broth, and dried thyme into the Instant Pot.
2) Close the lid, set to high pressure for 12 minutes, then allow natural pressure release for 5 minutes.
3) Serve after stirring gently.

Nutritional Information: (per serving)

Calories: 320 | Protein: 28g | Fat: 10g | Carbohydrates: 30g | Fiber: 4g

Tips:

- Add additional herbs like parsley for a flavor boost.
- Ensure beef cubes are evenly sized for consistent cooking.

15)   Beef and Chickpea Stew

Cook Time: 30 minutes

Servings: 4

Ingredients:

- 1 pound beef stew meat, cubed
- 1 can (15 oz) chickpeas, drained and rinsed
- 1 cup diced tomatoes
- 2 cups low-sodium beef broth
- 1 teaspoon cumin
- 1/2 teaspoon smoked paprika

Instructions:

1) Place beef, chickpeas, diced tomatoes, beef broth, cumin, and smoked paprika into

2) Close the lid, set to high pressure for 15 minutes, then perform a quick release.

3) Allow it to cool slightly before serving.

Nutritional Information: (per serving)

Calories: 340 | Protein: 26g | Fat: 10g | Carbohydrates: 30g | Fiber: 8g

Tips:

- Use smoked paprika for an added depth of flavor.
- Experiment with different types of beans for variety.

16) Beef and Barley Soup

Cook Time: 35 minutes

Servings: 5

Ingredients:

- 1 pound beef chuck roast, cubed
- 1 cup pearl barley, rinsed
- 4 cups low-sodium beef broth
- 1 carrot, diced
- 1 celery stalk, chopped
- 1 teaspoon dried thyme

Instructions:

1) Place beef, pearl barley, diced carrot, chopped celery, beef broth, and dried thyme into the Instant Pot.
2) Close the lid, set to high pressure for 20 minutes, then perform a quick release.
3) Stir gently before serving.

Nutritional Information: (per serving)

Calories: 380 | Protein: 30g | Fat: 12g | Carbohydrates: 35g | Fiber: 8g

Tips:

- Add a splash of Worcestershire sauce for added richness.
- Let the soup cool slightly before serving to avoid burns.

17) Beef and Cauliflower Curry

Cook Time: 25 minutes

Servings: 4

Ingredients:

- 1 pound beef stew meat, cubed
- 1 small head cauliflower, chopped
- 1 cup low-sodium beef broth
- 1 can (14 oz) coconut milk
- 1 tablespoon curry powder
- 1/2 teaspoon turmeric

Instructions:

1) Place beef, chopped cauliflower, beef broth, coconut milk, curry powder, and turmeric into the Instant Pot.
2) Close the lid, set to high pressure for 12 minutes, then perform a quick release.
3) Allow it to cool slightly before serving.

Nutritional Information: (per serving)

Calories: 320 | Protein: 28g | Fat: 14g | Carbohydrates: 20g | Fiber: 6g

Tips:

- Use lean cuts of beef to minimize fat content.
- Serve over a bed of cooked rice or quinoa for a complete meal.

18) Beef and Broccoli Stir-Fry

Cook Time: 15 minutes

Servings: 4

Ingredients:

- 1 pound beef sirloin, thinly sliced
- 2 cups broccoli florets
- 1 bell pepper, sliced
- 1/4 cup low-sodium soy sauce
- 2 tablespoons honey

Instructions:

1) Set the Instant Pot to sauté mode and brown beef slices.
2) Add broccoli florets, sliced bell pepper and soy sauce, honey
3) Close the lid, set to high pressure for 5 minutes, then perform a quick release.
4) Allow it to cool slightly before serving.

Nutritional Information: (per serving)

Calories: 280 | Protein: 26g | Fat: 8g | Carbohydrates: 20g | Fiber: 3g

Tips:

- Use low-sodium soy sauce for reduced sodium content.
- Stir-fry until vegetables are tender yet crisp for added texture.

19) Beef and Red Lentil Stew

Cook Time: 30 minutes

Servings: 4

Ingredients:

- 1 pound beef stew meat, cubed
- 1 cup red lentils, rinsed
- 2 cups low-sodium beef broth
- 1 teaspoon paprika
- 1/2 teaspoon cumin

Instructions:

1) Place beef, red lentils, beef broth, paprika, and cumin into the Instant Pot.
2) Close the lid, set to high pressure for 15 minutes, then perform a quick release.
3) Stir gently before serving.

Nutritional Information: (per serving)

Calories: 360 | Protein: 30g | Fat: 10g | Carbohydrates: 30g | Fiber: 12g

Tips:

- Adjust seasoning to suit your dog's taste buds.
- Red lentils cook quickly and provide added protein and fiber.

20) Beef and Green Bean Casserole

Cook Time: 20 minutes

Servings: 4

Ingredients:

- 1 pound beef stew meat, cubed
- 2 cups green beans, trimmed and halved
- 1 cup low-sodium beef broth
- 1/2 cup shredded cheese (optional)
- 1/4 teaspoon dried thyme

Instructions:

1) Place beef, green beans, beef broth, and dried thyme into the Instant Pot.
2) Close the lid, set to high pressure for 10 minutes, then perform a quick release.
3) Sprinkle shredded cheese (if using) over the casserole and allow it to melt before serving.

Nutritional Information: (per serving)

Calories: 320 | Protein: 28g | Fat: 10g | Carbohydrates: 25g | Fiber: 5g

Tips:

- Opt for low-fat cheese or skip it if your dog is sensitive to dairy.
- Steam green beans separately if your dog prefers a crunchier texture.

FISH AND SEAFOOD CREATIONS

21)   Tuna and Brown Rice Medley

Cook Time: 15 minutes

Servings: 4

Ingredients:

- 1 can (12 oz) tuna in water, drained
- 1 cup brown rice, rinsed
- 2 cups low-sodium vegetable broth
- 1 cup diced carrots
- 1/2 teaspoon dried parsley

Instructions:

1) Combine tuna, brown rice, vegetable broth, diced carrots, and dried parsley in the Instant Pot.
2) Close the lid, set to high pressure for 5 minutes, then perform a quick release.
3) Allow it to cool before serving.

Nutritional Information: (per serving)

Calories: 260 | Protein: 20g | Fat: 3g | Carbohydrates: 40g | Fiber: 5g

Tips:

- Add frozen peas for an extra burst of color and nutrients.
- Ensure rice is thoroughly cooked for easy digestion.

22) Salmon and Quinoa Pilaf

Cook Time: 20 minutes

Servings: 4

Ingredients:

- 1 pound salmon fillets, cut into chunks
- 1 cup quinoa, rinsed
- 2 cups low-sodium chicken broth
- 1 cup chopped spinach
- 1 teaspoon dried dill

Instructions:

1) Combine salmon chunks, quinoa, chicken broth, chopped spinach, and dried dill in the Instant Pot.
2) Close the lid, set to high pressure for 8 minutes, then allow natural pressure release for 5 minutes.
3) Fluff gently before serving.

Nutritional Information: (per serving)

Calories: 300 | Protein: 25g | Fat: 10g | Carbohydrates: 25g | Fiber: 4g

Tips:

- Use fresh dill for a more pronounced flavor.
- Substitute spinach with kale for added variety.

23) Shrimp and Vegetable Stir-Fry

Cook Time: 10 minutes

Servings: 4

Ingredients:

- 1/2 pound shrimp, peeled and deveined
- 2 cups mixed vegetables (bell peppers, snap peas, broccoli)
- 1/4 cup low-sodium soy sauce
- 2 tablespoons honey
- 1 tablespoon sesame oil

Instructions:

1) Sauté shrimp in sesame oil in the Instant Pot until pink.
2) Add mixed vegetables, soy sauce, and honey.
3) Close the lid, set to sauté mode for 3 minutes, stirring occasionally.

Nutritional Information: (per serving)

Calories: 180 | Protein: 15g | Fat: 4g | Carbohydrates: 20g | Fiber: 4g

Tips:

- Adjust honey for sweetness based on your dog's preference.
- Serve over cooked rice or quinoa for a complete meal.

24) Cod and Potato Stew

Cook Time: 18 minutes

Servings: 4

Ingredients:

- 1 pound cod fillets, cut into chunks
- 2 potatoes, peeled and diced
- 1 cup chopped tomatoes
- 2 cups low-sodium fish or vegetable broth
- 1/2 teaspoon dried thyme

Instructions:

1) Place cod chunks, diced potatoes, chopped tomatoes, fish broth, and dried thyme into the Instant Pot.
2) Close the lid, set to high pressure for 8 minutes, then perform a quick release.
3) Gently stir the stew before serving.

Nutritional Information: (per serving)

Calories: 220 | Protein: 20g | Fat: 1g | Carbohydrates: 30g | Fiber: 4g

Tips:

- Choose lean cod fillets for a healthier option.
- Add a sprinkle of fresh herbs for extra flavor.

25) Tuna and Brown Rice Congee

Cook Time: 25 minutes

Servings: 4

Ingredients:

- 1 can (12 oz) tuna in water, drained
- 1 cup brown rice, rinsed
- 4 cups low-sodium chicken broth
- 1 cup sliced shiitake mushrooms
- 1 tablespoon fresh cilantro, chopped

Instructions:

1) Combine tuna, brown rice, chicken broth, sliced shiitake mushrooms, and fresh cilantro in the Instant Pot.
2) Close the lid, set to high pressure for 15 minutes, then allow natural pressure release for 5 minutes.
3) Mix well before serving.

Nutritional Information: (per serving)

Calories: 280 | Protein: 22g | Fat: 2g | Carbohydrates: 45g | Fiber: 5g

Tips:

- Use short-grain brown rice for a creamier texture.
- Garnish with a squeeze of lime for added zest.

26)   Salmon and Green Bean Medley

Cook Time: 12 minutes

Servings: 4

Ingredients:

- 1 pound salmon fillets, cut into chunks
- 2 cups green beans, trimmed and halved
- 1 cup low-sodium vegetable broth
- 1 lemon, sliced
- 1/4 teaspoon dried rosemary

Instructions:

1) Place salmon chunks, green beans, vegetable broth, lemon slices, and dried rosemary into the Instant Pot.
2) Close the lid, set to high pressure for 5 minutes, then perform a quick release.
3) Allow it to cool slightly before serving.

Nutritional Information: (per serving)

Calories: 260 | Protein: 24g | Fat: 10g | Carbohydrates: 15g | Fiber: 5g

Tips:

- Opt for wild-caught salmon for higher omega-3 content.
- Remove lemon slices before serving if your dog prefers.

27) Shrimp and Tomato Pasta

Cook Time: 8 minutes

Servings: 4

Ingredients:

- 1/2 pound shrimp, peeled and deveined
- 8 oz whole wheat or gluten-free pasta
- 2 cups low-sodium vegetable broth
- 1 cup diced tomatoes
- 2 tablespoons olive oil

Instructions:

1) Sauté shrimp in olive oil in the Instant Pot until pink.
2) Add pasta, vegetable broth, and diced tomatoes.
3) Close the lid, set to high pressure for 4 minutes, then perform a quick release.
4) Mix gently before serving.

Nutritional Information: (per serving)

Calories: 230 | Protein: 18g | Fat: 4g | Carbohydrates: 35g | Fiber: 5g

Tips:

- Use whole wheat or gluten-free pasta for a healthier option.
- Rinse pasta after cooking to remove excess starch.

28) Cod and Spinach Soup

Cook Time: 15 minutes

Servings: 4

Ingredients:

- 1 pound cod fillets, cut into chunks
- 4 cups low-sodium vegetable broth
- 2 cups fresh spinach leaves
- 1 teaspoon dried basil

Instructions:

1) Place cod chunks, vegetable broth, fresh spinach leaves, and dried basil into the Instant Pot.
2) Close the lid, set to high pressure for 6 minutes, then perform a quick release.
3) Gently stir the soup before serving.

Nutritional Information: (per serving)

Calories: 180 | Protein: 22g | Fat: 1g | Carbohydrates: 15g | Fiber: 4g

Tips:

- Use baby spinach for a milder flavor.
- Adjust seasoning to suit your dog's taste preferences.

29)   Salmon and Broccoli Stir-Fry

Cook Time: 10 minutes

Servings: 4

Ingredients:

- 1 pound salmon fillets, cut into chunks
- 2 cups broccoli florets
- 1 bell pepper, sliced
- 1/4 cup low-sodium soy sauce
- 2 tablespoons honey
- 1 tablespoon olive oil

Instructions:

1) Sauté salmon chunks in olive oil in the Instant Pot until cooked.
2) Add broccoli florets, sliced bell pepper, soy sauce, and honey.
3) Close the lid, set to sauté mode for 3 minutes, stirring occasionally.

Nutritional Information: (per serving)

Calories: 270 | Protein: 22g | Fat: 10g | Carbohydrates: 20g | Fiber: 4g

Tips:

- Choose fresh, firm broccoli for better texture.
- Adjust honey according to your dog's taste preferences.

30)   Cod and Cauliflower Curry

Cook Time: 20 minutes

Servings: 4

Ingredients:

- 1 pound cod fillets, cut into chunks
- 1 head cauliflower, chopped into florets
- 1 can (14 oz) coconut milk
- 2 teaspoons curry powder
- 1/2 teaspoon turmeric

Instructions:

1) Place cod chunks, cauliflower florets, coconut milk, curry powder, and turmeric into the Instant Pot.
2) Close the lid, set to high pressure for 8 minutes, then perform a quick release.
3) Allow it to cool slightly before serving.

Nutritional Information: (per serving)

Calories: 280 | Protein: 24g | Fat: 15g | Carbohydrates: 15g | Fiber: 5g

Tips:

- Use light coconut milk for a lighter option.
- Serve with a side of rice or quinoa for a complete meal.

VEGETARIAN AND VEGAN OPTIONS

31)   Lentil and Sweet Potato Stew

Cook Time: 20 minutes

Servings: 4

Ingredients:

- 1 cup dried green or brown lentils
- 2 sweet potatoes, peeled and diced
- 1 can (14 oz) diced tomatoes
- 4 cups low-sodium vegetable broth
- 1 teaspoon dried thyme

Instructions:

1) Combine lentils, diced sweet potatoes, diced tomatoes, vegetable broth, and dried thyme in the Instant Pot.
2) Close the lid, set to high pressure for 10 minutes, then allow natural pressure release for 5 minutes.
3) Mix well before serving.

Nutritional Information: (per serving)

Calories: 280 | Protein: 15g | Fat: 1g | Carbohydrates: 55g | Fiber: 15g

Tips:

- Add chopped kale or spinach for extra nutrition.
- Mash slightly for a thicker consistency.

32) Vegan Chickpea Curry

Cook Time: 15 minutes

Servings: 4

Ingredients:

- 2 cans (15 oz each) chickpeas, drained and rinsed
- 1 can (14 oz) coconut milk
- 2 cups diced bell peppers (various colors)
- 2 tablespoons curry powder

Instructions:

1) Combine chickpeas, coconut milk, diced bell peppers, and curry powder in the Instant Pot.
2) Close the lid, set to high pressure for 5 minutes, then perform a quick release.
3) Allow it to cool slightly before serving.

Nutritional Information: (per serving)

Calories: 320 | Protein: 12g | Fat: 15g | Carbohydrates: 40g | Fiber: 10g

Tips:

- Customize spice levels according to your dog's preference.
- Serve with a side of cooked rice or quinoa.

33) Quinoa and Mixed Vegetable Pilaf

Cook Time: 12 minutes

Servings: 4

Ingredients:

- 1 cup quinoa, rinsed
- 2 cups mixed vegetables (carrots, peas, corn)
- 2 cups low-sodium vegetable broth
- 1 teaspoon dried parsley

Instructions:

1) Combine quinoa, mixed vegetables, vegetable broth, and dried parsley in the Instant Pot.
2) Close the lid, set to high pressure for 5 minutes, then allow natural pressure release for 5 minutes.
3) Fluff gently before serving.

Nutritional Information: (per serving)

Calories: 230 | Protein: 8g | Fat: 3g | Carbohydrates: 45g | Fiber: 7g

Tips:

- Use frozen mixed vegetables for convenience.
- Add a splash of lemon juice for a zesty flavor.

34) Vegan Black Bean Chili

Cook Time: 20 minutes

Servings: 4

Ingredients:

- 2 cans (15 oz each) black beans, drained and rinsed
- 1 can (14 oz) diced tomatoes
- 2 cups vegetable broth
- 2 teaspoons chili powder

Instructions:

1) Combine black beans, diced tomatoes, vegetable broth, and chili powder in the Instant Pot.
2) Close the lid, set to high pressure for 10 minutes, then perform a quick release.
3) Stir well before serving.

Nutritional Information: (per serving)

Calories: 260 | Protein: 15g | Fat: 1g | Carbohydrates: 50g | Fiber: 15g

Tips:

- Customize spice levels to suit your dog's taste.
- Top with a dollop of dairy-free yogurt for added creaminess (if your dog tolerates dairy).

35) Vegan Split Pea Soup

Cook Time: 25 minutes

Servings: 4

Ingredients:

- 1 cup green split peas, rinsed
- 2 carrots, sliced
- 4 cups low-sodium vegetable broth
- 1 teaspoon dried thyme

Instructions:

1) Combine green split peas, sliced carrots, vegetable broth, and dried thyme in the Instant Pot.
2) Close the lid, set to high pressure for 15 minutes, then allow natural pressure release for 5 minutes.
3) Mix well before serving.

Nutritional Information: (per serving)

Calories: 240 | Protein: 10g | Fat: 1g | Carbohydrates: 45g | Fiber: 15g

Tips:

- Purée for a smoother texture if desired.
- Add a squeeze of lemon juice for brightness.

36) Vegan Lentil and Mushroom Risotto

Cook Time: 18 minutes

Servings: 4

Ingredients:

- 1 cup green or brown lentils, rinsed
- 1 cup sliced mushrooms
- 2 cups vegetable broth
- 1 cup Arborio rice

Instructions:

1) Combine lentils, sliced mushrooms, vegetable broth, and Arborio rice in the Instant Pot.
2) Close the lid, set to high pressure for 8 minutes, then perform a quick release.
3) Stir gently before serving.

Nutritional Information: (per serving)

Calories: 290 | Protein: 15g | Fat: 1g | Carbohydrates: 55g | Fiber: 15g

Tips:

- Use a mix of mushroom varieties for enhanced flavor.
- Garnish with fresh parsley for a finishing touch.

37) Vegan Tomato Basil Pasta

Cook Time: 10 minutes

Servings: 4

Ingredients:

- 8 oz pasta (whole wheat or gluten-free)
- 1 can (14 oz) diced tomatoes
- 2 cups low-sodium vegetable broth
- 1 teaspoon dried basil
- 1 tablespoon olive oil

Instructions:

1) Combine pasta, diced tomatoes, vegetable broth, dried basil, and olive oil in the Instant Pot.
2) Close the lid, set to high pressure for 4 minutes, then perform a quick release.
3) Mix well before serving.

Nutritional Information: (per serving)

Calories: 270 | Protein: 8g | Fat: 4g | Carbohydrates: 50g | Fiber: 5g

Tips:

- Add chopped spinach or kale for added nutrients.
- Stir in a teaspoon of nutritional yeast for a cheesy flavor.

38) Vegan Red Lentil Soup

Cook Time: 15 minutes

Servings: 4

Ingredients:

- 1 cup red lentils, rinsed
- 2 carrots, sliced
- 4 cups low-sodium vegetable broth
- 1 teaspoon ground cumin

Instructions:

1) Combine red lentils, sliced carrots, vegetable broth, and ground cumin in the Instant Pot.
2) Close the lid, set to high pressure for 8 minutes, then perform a quick release.
3) Stir well before serving.

Nutritional Information: (per serving)

Calories: 230 | Protein: 10g | Fat: 1g | Carbohydrates: 40g | Fiber: 15g

Tips:

- Purée for a smoother consistency if preferred.
- Garnish with a dollop of dairy-free yogurt for extra creaminess.

39)   Butternut Squash Risotto

Cook Time: 22 minutes

Servings: 4

Ingredients:

- 2 cups diced butternut squash
- 1 cup Arborio rice
- 4 cups low-sodium vegetable broth

Instructions:

1) Combine diced butternut squash, Arborio rice, and vegetable broth in the Instant Pot.
2) Close the lid, set to high pressure for 10 minutes, then perform a quick release.
3) Stir gently before serving.

Nutritional Information: (per serving)

Calories: 260 | Protein: 6g | Fat: 3g | Carbohydrates: 50g | Fiber: 6g

Tips:

- Use pre-cut butternut squash for convenience.
- Garnish with a sprinkle of fresh sage for added flavor.

40)   Mushroom and Barley Stew

Cook Time: 25 minutes

Servings: 4

Ingredients:

- 1 cup pearl barley, rinsed
- 2 cups sliced mushrooms
- 4 cups low-sodium vegetable broth
- 1 teaspoon dried thyme

Instructions:

1) Combine pearl barley, sliced mushrooms, vegetable broth, and dried thyme in the Instant Pot.
2) Close the lid, set to high pressure for 15 minutes, then allow natural pressure release for 5 minutes.
3) Mix well before serving.

Nutritional Information: (per serving)

Calories: 280 | Protein: 10g | Fat: 1g | Carbohydrates: 60g | Fiber: 10g

Tips:

- Add diced potatoes for extra heartiness.
- Season with a splash of balsamic vinegar for depth of flavor.

CHAPTER 4
SPECIAL DIETS AND HEALTH CONCERNS

RECIPES FOR DOGS WITH ALLERGIES

41) Turkey and Sweet Potato Mash

Cook Time: 20 minutes

Servings: 4

Ingredients:

- 1 pound ground turkey
- 2 sweet potatoes, peeled and diced
- 2 cups low-sodium chicken or turkey broth
- 1 teaspoon dried parsley

Instructions:

1) Brown ground turkey in the Instant Pot using the sauté function.
2) Add diced sweet potatoes, broth, and dried parsley.
3) Close the lid, set to high pressure for 8 minutes, then perform a quick release.
4) Mash gently before serving.

Nutritional Information: (per serving)

Calories: 250 | Protein: 20g | Fat: 8g | Carbohydrates: 20g | Fiber: 4g

Tips:

- Use lean ground turkey for lower fat content.
- Cool thoroughly before serving to avoid burning your dog's mouth.

42)   Salmon and Pumpkin Medley

Cook Time: 10 minutes

Servings: 4

Ingredients:

- 1 pound salmon fillets, cut into chunks
- 2 cups diced pumpkin or butternut squash
- 2 cups low-sodium vegetable or fish broth

Instructions:

1) Place salmon chunks, diced pumpkin, and broth in the Instant Pot.
2) Close the lid, set to high pressure for 5 minutes, then perform a quick release.
3) Flake the salmon and mix gently before serving.

Nutritional Information: (per serving)

Calories: 230 | Protein: 22g | Fat: 10g | Carbohydrates: 10g | Fiber: 3g

Tips:

- Remove salmon skin before cooking.
- Ensure the pumpkin or squash is soft enough for easy digestion.

43) Beef and Carrot Stew

Cook Time: 25 minutes

Servings: 4

Ingredients:

- 1 pound beef stew meat, cut into small pieces
- 2 cups diced carrots
- 2 cups low-sodium beef broth
- 1 tablespoon olive oil

Instructions:

1) Sear beef pieces in olive oil using the sauté function.
2) Add diced carrots and beef broth to the Instant Pot.
3) Close the lid, set to high pressure for 15 minutes, then perform a quick release.
4) Allow it to cool before serving.

Nutritional Information: (per serving)

Calories: 280 | Protein: 24g | Fat: 12g | Carbohydrates: 12g | Fiber: 3g

Tips:

- Trim excess fat from the beef.
- Cut carrots into smaller pieces for easier consumption.

44) Chicken and Brown Rice Porridge

Cook Time: 15 minutes

Servings: 4

Ingredients:

- 1 pound boneless, skinless chicken thighs, diced
- 1 cup brown rice
- 4 cups low-sodium chicken broth

Instructions:

1) Combine diced chicken, brown rice, and chicken broth in the Instant Pot.
2) Close the lid, set to high pressure for 10 minutes, then perform a quick release.
3) Stir well before serving.

Nutritional Information: (per serving)

Calories: 320 | Protein: 28g | Fat: 5g | Carbohydrates: 30g | Fiber: 2g

Tips:

- Use boneless chicken for easier digestion.
- Ensure the rice is fully cooked for better digestion.

45)   Lamb and Quinoa Stew

Cook Time: 20 minutes

Servings: 4

Ingredients:

- 1 pound lamb stew meat, diced
- 1 cup quinoa, rinsed
- 2 cups low-sodium lamb or vegetable broth

Instructions:

1) Brown lamb meat in the Instant Pot using the sauté function.
2) Add quinoa and broth to the pot.
3) Close the lid, set to high pressure for 8 minutes, then allow natural pressure release for 5 minutes.
4) Mix gently before serving.

Nutritional Information: (per serving)

Calories: 290 | Protein: 24g | Fat: 14g | Carbohydrates: 20g | Fiber: 2g

Tips:

- Choose lean lamb cuts to reduce fat content.
- Ensure the quinoa is fully cooked before serving.

46) Turkey and Rice Congee

Cook Time: 25 minutes

Servings: 4

Ingredients:

- 1 pound ground turkey
- 1 cup white rice
- 4 cups low-sodium chicken or turkey broth

Instructions:

1) Brown ground turkey in the Instant Pot using the sauté function.
2) Add white rice and broth to the pot.
3) Close the lid, set to high pressure for 15 minutes, then perform a quick release.
4) Stir thoroughly before serving.

Nutritional Information: (per serving)

Calories: 280 | Protein: 20g | Fat: 10g | Carbohydrates: 25g | Fiber: 1g

Tips:

- Opt for ground turkey with a lower fat content.
- Allow the congee to cool adequately before feeding your dog.

47) Duck and Vegetable Casserole

Cook Time: 30 minutes

Servings: 4

Ingredients:

- 1 pound duck breast, diced
- 2 cups mixed vegetables (peas, carrots, green beans)
- 2 cups low-sodium vegetable or duck broth

Instructions:

1) Sear diced duck breast in the Instant Pot using the sauté function.
2) Add mixed vegetables and broth to the pot.
3) Close the lid, set to high pressure for 15 minutes, then perform a quick release.
4) Mix gently before serving.

Nutritional Information: (per serving)

Calories: 240 | Protein: 26g | Fat: 12g | Carbohydrates: 10g | Fiber: 3g

Tips:

- Remove excess skin from the duck.
- Ensure the duck is cooked through before serving.

WEIGHT MANAGEMENT MEALS

48) Turkey and Green Bean Stew

Cook Time: 25 minutes

Servings: 4

Ingredients:

- 1 pound ground turkey
- 2 cups fresh or frozen green beans
- 2 cups low-sodium chicken or turkey broth

Instructions:

1) Brown ground turkey in the Instant Pot using the sauté function.
2) Add green beans and broth to the pot.
3) Close the lid, set to high pressure for 10 minutes, then perform a quick release.
4) Mix thoroughly before serving.

Nutritional Information: (per serving)

Calories: 240 | Protein: 20g | Fat: 10g | Carbohydrates: 15g | Fiber: 5g

Tips:

- Opt for lean ground turkey for lower fat content.
- Cut green beans into bite-sized pieces for easier digestion.

49) Chicken and Spinach Stew

Cook Time: 20 minutes

Servings: 4

Ingredients:

- 1 pound boneless, skinless chicken thighs, diced
- 2 cups fresh spinach leaves
- 2 cups low-sodium chicken broth

Instructions:

1) Combine diced chicken, spinach, and chicken broth in the Instant Pot.
2) Close the lid, set to high pressure for 8 minutes, then perform a quick release.
3) Stir well before serving.

Nutritional Information: (per serving)

Calories: 260 | Protein: 24g | Fat: 10g | Carbohydrates: 10g | Fiber: 3g

Tips:

- Remove excess fat from the chicken before cooking.
- Use fresh spinach for maximum nutritional value.

50) Turkey and Pumpkin Stew

Cook Time: 20 minutes

Servings: 4

Ingredients:

- 1 pound ground turkey
- 2 cups diced pumpkin or butternut squash
- 2 cups low-sodium turkey or vegetable broth

Instructions:

1) Brown ground turkey in the Instant Pot using the sauté function.
2) Add diced pumpkin and broth to the pot.
3) Close the lid, set to high pressure for 8 minutes, then perform a quick release.
4) Mash slightly before serving.

Nutritional Information: (per serving)

Calories: 230 | Protein: 20g | Fat: 8g | Carbohydrates: 15g | Fiber: 4g

Tips:

- Use lean ground turkey for a healthier option.
- Ensure the pumpkin or squash is cooked until tender.

51) Chicken and Carrot Stew

Cook Time: 25 minutes

Servings: 4

Ingredients:

- 1 pound boneless, skinless chicken breasts, diced
- 2 cups diced carrots
- 2 cups low-sodium chicken broth

Instructions:

1) Combine diced chicken, carrots, and chicken broth in the Instant Pot.
2) Close the lid, set to high pressure for 10 minutes, then perform a quick release.
3) Mix well before serving.

Nutritional Information: (per serving)

Calories: 250 | Protein: 26g | Fat: 8g | Carbohydrates: 15g | Fiber: 4g

Tips:

- Trim visible fat from the chicken for a leaner meal.
- Chop carrots finely for easier consumption.

52)   Fish and Sweet Potato Medley

Cook Time: 15 minutes

Servings: 4

Ingredients:

- 1 pound white fish fillets (e.g., cod, haddock), cut into chunks
- 2 sweet potatoes, peeled and diced
- 2 cups low-sodium fish or vegetable broth

Instructions:

1) Place fish chunks, diced sweet potatoes, and broth in the Instant Pot.
2) Close the lid, set to high pressure for 5 minutes, then perform a quick release.
3) Flake the fish and mix gently before serving.

Nutritional Information: (per serving)

Calories: 220 | Protein: 24g | Fat: 4g | Carbohydrates: 20g | Fiber: 3g

Tips:

- Use a mild-flavored fish suitable for dogs.
- Ensure the sweet potatoes are soft enough for easy digestion.

53)   Lean Beef and Veggie Stew

Cook Time: 25 minutes

Servings: 4

Ingredients:

- 1 pound lean beef stew meat, diced
- 2 cups mixed vegetables (zucchini, broccoli, carrots)
- 2 cups low-sodium beef or vegetable broth

Instructions:

1) Brown beef stew meat in the Instant Pot using the sauté function.
2) Add mixed vegetables and broth to the pot.
3) Close the lid, set to high pressure for 10 minutes, then perform a quick release.
4) Allow it to cool slightly before serving.

Nutritional Information: (per serving)

Calories: 240 | Protein: 28g | Fat: 10g | Carbohydrates: 15g | Fiber: 5g

Tips:

- Remove excess fat from the beef before cooking.
- Cut vegetables into small pieces for easier consumption.

54) Chicken and Quinoa Pilaf

Cook Time: 18 minutes

Servings: 4

Ingredients:

- 1 pound boneless, skinless chicken breasts, diced
- 1 cup quinoa, rinsed
- 2 cups low-sodium chicken broth

Instructions:

1) Combine diced chicken, quinoa, and chicken broth in the Instant Pot.
2) Close the lid, set to high pressure for 8 minutes, then perform a quick release.
3) Fluff gently before serving.

Nutritional Information: (per serving)

Calories: 280 | Protein: 26g | Fat: 6g | Carbohydrates: 25g | Fiber: 3g

Tips:

- Use boneless chicken for easier digestion.
- Ensure the quinoa is fully cooked before serving.

55) Turkey and Barley Stew

Cook Time: 20 minutes

Servings: 4

Ingredients:

- 1 pound ground turkey
- 1 cup pearl barley, rinsed
- 2 cups low-sodium turkey or vegetable broth

Instructions:

1) Brown ground turkey in the Instant Pot using the sauté function.
2) Add pearl barley and broth to the pot.
3) Close the lid, set to high pressure for 8 minutes, then allow natural pressure release for 5 minutes.
4) Stir well before serving.

Nutritional Information: (per serving)

Calories: 240 | Protein: 22g | Fat: 8g | Carbohydrates: 20g | Fiber: 5g

Tips:

- Opt for lean ground turkey for lower fat content.
- Ensure the barley is fully cooked before serving.

SENIOR DOG NUTRITION

56) Chicken and Brown Rice Stew

Cook Time: 20 minutes

Servings: 4

Ingredients:

- 1 pound boneless, skinless chicken thighs, diced
- 1 cup brown rice
- 3 cups low-sodium chicken broth

Instructions:

1) Combine diced chicken, brown rice, and chicken broth in the Instant Pot.
2) Close the lid, set to high pressure for 10 minutes, then perform a quick release.
3) Stir gently before serving.

Nutritional Information: (per serving)

Calories: 260 | Protein: 24g | Fat: 8g | Carbohydrates: 20g | Fiber: 2g

Tips:

- Use boneless chicken for easier digestion.
- Ensure the rice is fully cooked for better digestibility.

57) Turkey and Sweet Potato Casserole

Cook Time: 25 minutes

Servings: 4

Ingredients:

- 1 pound ground turkey
- 2 sweet potatoes, peeled and diced
- 2 cups low-sodium turkey or vegetable broth

Instructions:

1) Brown ground turkey in the Instant Pot using the sauté function.
2) Add diced sweet potatoes and broth to the pot.
3) Close the lid, set to high pressure for 8 minutes, then perform a quick release.
4) Mash gently before serving.

Nutritional Information: (per serving)

Calories: 240 | Protein: 20g | Fat: 8g | Carbohydrates: 20g | Fiber: 3g

Tips:

- Opt for lean ground turkey for lower fat content.
- Ensure sweet potatoes are soft for easier digestion.

58)   Beef and Barley Stew

Cook Time: 25 minutes

Servings: 4

Ingredients:

- 1 pound beef stew meat, diced
- 1 cup pearl barley, rinsed
- 3 cups low-sodium beef broth

Instructions:

1) Brown beef stew meat in the Instant Pot using the sauté function.
2) Add pearl barley and broth to the pot.
3) Close the lid, set to high pressure for 12 minutes, then allow natural pressure release for 5 minutes.
4) Stir well before serving.

Nutritional Information: (per serving)

Calories: 280 | Protein: 26g | Fat: 10g | Carbohydrates: 20g | Fiber: 5g

Tips:

- Trim excess fat from the beef for a leaner meal.
- Ensure the barley is fully cooked before serving.

59) Salmon and Vegetable Medley

Cook Time: 15 minutes

Servings: 4

Ingredients:

- 1 pound salmon fillets, cut into chunks
- 2 cups mixed vegetables (carrots, green beans, peas)
- 2 cups low-sodium vegetable or fish broth

Instructions:

1) Place salmon chunks, mixed vegetables, and broth in the Instant Pot.
2) Close the lid, set to high pressure for 5 minutes, then perform a quick release.
3) Flake the salmon and mix gently before serving.

Nutritional Information: (per serving)

Calories: 240 | Protein: 24g | Fat: 12g | Carbohydrates: 15g | Fiber: 4g

Tips:

- Remove salmon skin before cooking.
- Use boneless and skinless salmon for easier digestion.

60) Chicken and Quinoa Porridge

Cook Time: 18 minutes

Servings: 4

Ingredients:

- 1 pound boneless, skinless chicken breasts, diced
- 1 cup quinoa, rinsed
- 3 cups low-sodium chicken broth

Instructions:

1) Combine diced chicken, quinoa, and chicken broth in the Instant Pot.
2) Close the lid, set to high pressure for 10 minutes, then perform a quick release.
3) Fluff gently before serving.

Nutritional Information: (per serving)

Calories: 280 | Protein: 26g | Fat: 6g | Carbohydrates: 25g | Fiber: 3g

Tips:

- Use boneless chicken for easier digestion.
- Ensure the quinoa is fully cooked before serving.

61) Lamb and Vegetable Stew

Cook Time: 25 minutes

Servings: 4

Ingredients:

- 1 pound lamb stew meat, diced
- 2 cups mixed vegetables (potatoes, carrots, green beans)
- 3 cups low-sodium lamb or vegetable broth

Instructions:

1) Brown lamb meat in the Instant Pot using the sauté function.
2) Add mixed vegetables and broth to the pot.
3) Close the lid, set to high pressure for 12 minutes, then perform a quick release.
4) Allow it to cool slightly before serving.

Nutritional Information: (per serving)

Calories: 280 | Protein: 24g | Fat: 12g | Carbohydrates: 20g | Fiber: 4g

Tips:

- Choose lean cuts of lamb to reduce fat content.
- Cut vegetables into bite-sized pieces for easier consumption.

62) Turkey and Pumpkin Stew

Cook Time: 20 minutes

Servings: 4

Ingredients:

- 1 pound ground turkey
- 2 cups diced pumpkin or butternut squash
- 3 cups low-sodium turkey or vegetable broth

Instructions:

1) Brown ground turkey in the Instant Pot using the sauté function.
2) Add diced pumpkin and broth to the pot.
3) Close the lid, set to high pressure for 8 minutes, then perform a quick release.
4) Mash slightly before serving.

Nutritional Information: (per serving)

Calories: 240 | Protein: 20g | Fat: 8g | Carbohydrates: 20g | Fiber: 4g

Tips:

- Opt for lean ground turkey for a healthier option.
- Ensure the pumpkin or squash is cooked until tender.

63) Beef and Vegetable Rice

Cook Time: 25 minutes

Servings: 4

Ingredients:

- 1 pound beef stew meat, diced
- 1 cup brown rice
- 3 cups low-sodium beef broth

Instructions:

1) Brown beef stew meat in the Instant Pot using the sauté function.
2) Add brown rice and broth to the pot.
3) Close the lid, set to high pressure for 12 minutes, then allow natural pressure release for 5 minutes.
4) Stir well before serving.

Nutritional Information: (per serving)

Calories: 280 | Protein: 26g | Fat: 10g | Carbohydrates: 20g | Fiber: 3g

Tips:

- Trim excess fat from the beef for a leaner meal.
- Ensure the rice is fully cooked before serving.

CHAPTER 5

MEAL PLANNING AND STORAGE

When it comes to ensuring your furry friend receives the best nutrition, meal planning and proper storage techniques play a vital role. In this chapter, we'll delve into the art of batch cooking for convenience, effective ways to store homemade dog meals, and how to create a balanced weekly meal plan tailored to your dog's needs.

BATCH COOKING FOR CONVENIENCE

Why Batch Cooking?

Imagine having ready-to-serve meals for your canine companion without the hassle of daily cooking. Batch cooking allows you to prepare larger quantities of dog food in a single cooking session, saving you time throughout the week. It's a game-changer for busy pet owners seeking convenience without compromising on quality.

Optimizing Your Instant Pot

Your Instant Pot becomes an indispensable tool for batch cooking. Its efficiency in preparing large portions of dog food swiftly and with minimal effort is unmatched. Utilize its various settings to prepare different recipes in batches, from proteins like chicken and beef to grains and vegetables.

Meal Prep Tips

Before starting your batch cooking session, plan the recipes you want to prepare for the week. Ensure you have all the necessary ingredients on hand. Prepare your kitchen by organizing utensils, cutting boards, and containers for storage. Consider using separate utensils and tools exclusively for your dog's meals to prevent cross-contamination.

Time-Saving Techniques

Utilize time-saving techniques such as pre-cutting vegetables, portioning ingredients, and pre-measuring spices and supplements. This not only streamlines the cooking process but also makes it easier to monitor the nutritional content of each meal.

Cooking in Batches

Prepare larger quantities of dog food in your Instant Pot by adjusting ingredient proportions accordingly. Utilize the "Saute" function for browning meats and the "Pressure Cook" function for simmering stews and grains. Consider multitasking by cooking different components simultaneously, saving both time and energy.

PROPER STORAGE AND FREEZING TIPS

Choosing the Right Containers

Selecting the appropriate storage containers is crucial to maintain freshness and prevent spoilage. Opt for airtight containers made of glass or BPA-free plastic. Ensure the containers are specifically designated for your dog's food to avoid any cross-contamination risks.

Portion Control

Divide the batch-cooked food into individual portions suitable for your dog's daily intake. Portion control helps manage your dog's weight and ensures consistent meal sizes. Use measuring cups or a food scale to accurately portion meals.

Refrigeration Guidelines

Once the cooked food has cooled completely, refrigerate portions immediately. Refrigeration maintains freshness for a few days, typically up to three to four days, depending on the ingredients used. Label containers with the date to track freshness.

Freezing Techniques

For longer storage, freezing is your best friend. Use freezer-safe containers or resealable freezer bags to store portions. Ensure to remove excess air from bags to prevent freezer burn. Frozen homemade dog food can typically be stored for up to three months.

Thawing Safely

When ready to serve, thaw frozen dog food portions in the refrigerator overnight. Avoid thawing dog food at room temperature to prevent bacterial growth. Use thawed portions within 24 to 48 hours and discard any leftovers to maintain freshness and quality.

CREATING A BALANCED WEEKLY MEAL PLAN

Understanding Nutritional Needs

Designing a balanced meal plan requires understanding your dog's specific nutritional requirements. Consider factors such as age, weight, activity level, and any dietary restrictions or health conditions your dog may have. Consult with your veterinarian to determine the ideal nutritional profile for your furry friend.

Variety in Ingredients

Incorporating a variety of ingredients ensures your dog receives a spectrum of nutrients. Plan meals that include a balance of proteins (meat, fish), carbohydrates (rice, quinoa), and vegetables (carrots, green beans). Rotate ingredients to provide diversity in flavors and nutrients.

Meal Rotation Strategy

Implement a meal rotation strategy to prevent dietary monotony and potential nutritional deficiencies. Rotate between different recipes throughout the week or month to offer a diverse range of nutrients and flavors while keeping mealtime exciting for your dog.

Tracking and Adjusting

Maintain a log or journal to track the meals served to your dog. Monitor your dog's response to different recipes, noting any digestive issues, allergies, or changes in energy levels or coat condition. Use this information to fine-tune the meal plan to best suit your dog's needs.

CONCLUSION

Congratulations on reaching the end of this nourishing adventure through the pages of our Instant Pot dog food cookbook! You've embarked on a journey that transcends mere mealtimes—it's a commitment to the well-being and vitality of your beloved furry friend.

Throughout this cookbook, we've unveiled the magic of the Instant Pot as a culinary powerhouse for crafting wholesome and nutritious meals tailored specifically for your dog. From sumptuous stews to delightful casseroles, each recipe is a testament to our dedication to providing easy, vet-approved, and lip-smackingly delicious meals for your furry companion.

Yet, this is merely a stepping stone toward a vibrant and healthier life for your dog. Your feedback is not just welcomed; it's cherished! Your experiences, triumphs, and even your challenges are vital to us. Your input guides us in our mission to continually enhance and cater to the diverse needs of every dog and their devoted human.

We urge you to let your voice be heard. Share your victories, your journey through these recipes, and the heartwarming joy that glows in your dog's eyes after savoring a homemade meal. Your stories fuel our passion to improve, innovate, and foster a community committed to the well-being of our canine companions.

Remember, each dog is unique. Experiment, tweak, and personalize these recipes to suit your dog's individual palate and dietary requirements. Your feedback not only shapes the future editions of this cookbook but also cultivates a community united by our shared love for our furry family members.

Let's forge ahead together on this paws-itively fantastic adventure! Join us in celebrating the love, joy, and laughter our dogs bring into our lives. Share your anecdotes, snapshots of precious moments, and your invaluable feedback on our platform.

Together, we create more than just recipes; we create bonds, memories, and a haven for dog lovers alike. Thank you for choosing to nourish your dog with homemade meals crafted with love and care. Your unwavering commitment to their well-being inspires us all.

So, as we bid adieu for now, remember: every meal is an opportunity to shower your furry friend with love and health. Let's continue this journey, making a difference in the lives of our beloved dogs, one nutritious and delicious meal at a time.

BONUS: 30 DAY MEAL PLAN

DAY	MEAL
Day 1	Chicken and Brown Rice Stew
Day 2	Turkey and Sweet Potato Casserole
Day 3	Beef and Barley Stew
Day 4	Salmon and Vegetable Medley
Day 5	Chicken and Quinoa Porridge
Day 6	Lamb and Vegetable Stew
Day 7	Turkey and Pumpkin Stew
Day 8	Chicken and Green Bean Medley
Day 9	Beef and Carrot Stew
Day 10	Fish and Sweet Potato Delight
Day 11	Chicken and Spinach Delight
Day 12	Beef and Broccoli Casserole
Day 13	Turkey and Pumpkin Mash
Day 14	Chicken and Pea Stew
Day 15	Beef and Zucchini Medley
Day 16	Salmon and Carrot Casserole
Day 17	Turkey and Brown Rice Delight
Day 18	Chicken and Cauliflower Stew
Day 19	Beef and Potato Medley
Day 20	Fish and Green Bean Casserole

Day 21	Chicken and Carrot Medley
Day 22	Lamb and Sweet Potato Stew
Day 23	Turkey and Spinach Casserole
Day 24	Beef and Butternut Squash Stew
Day 25	Chicken and Tomato Delight
Day 26	Fish and Pea Medley
Day 27	Beef and Pumpkin Stew
Day 28	Turkey and Broccoli Casserole
Day 29	Chicken and Potato Mash
Day 30	Salmon and Zucchini Medley

Made in United States
Troutdale, OR
10/05/2024

23444048R00058